This book belongs to:

Written by:

MUJAWIYERA Eugenie

Illustrated by:

RUTAYISIRE Chris

I would like to thank Roxanna K., Joy M.,
Elvis M., and Molo M., who helped me
create this
amazing book.
You are awesome!

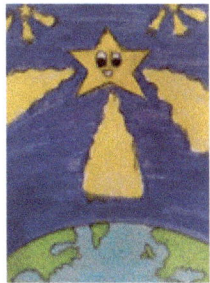

1

Bill and Roxanna's mothers are childhood friends and neighbours.

One day, there was no school, Bill and his mother went to Roxanna's house.

Bill: Hello Roxanna.

Roxanna: Hi Bill! Welcome to my home! Come, I am going to show you my books and we can read together. Bill, do you like reading?

Bill: I rarely read.

Roxanna: Why?

Bill: It's not fun.

Roxanna: Is it because you don't have any interesting books at home?

Bill: I do not have any books at all at home.

Roxanna: What? You do not have any books at home?

Bill: No.

Roxanna: How are you still alive?

Bill: It seems to me that you like to read because you have a lot of books at home.

9

Roxanna: Oh yes, I love to read! For me, reading is a lot of fun.

Bill: Why?

Roxanna: It is because in books there are different worlds.

Bill: Different worlds?

11

Roxanna: Yes, like in the animal books I like to read, the animals live in their own world!

Bill: That is not possible!

Roxanna: Yes, it is possible.

Bill: Beautiful! Where can we find good books about animals?

Roxanna: You can find them at different places like: the school library, public library or in bookstores that sell books.

Bill: How many books can you read per week?

Roxanna: I can read three books a week, which means a book can have between twenty-five to thirty pages.

Bill: That's right! How many minutes do you take each day to read?

15

Roxanna: I take fifteen to thirty minutes a day to read.

Bill: What time of day do you like to read?

Roxanna: In the morning at school or at night before going to sleep.

Bill: Way to go! You really are a great reader.

Roxanna: Thank you! Do you know that reading is very important in life?

Bill: Why? Can you explain?

Roxanna: Sure! I am going to tell you how reading has an incredible wealth:

When we read a lot, we improve our reading. Reading helps us to enrich our vocabulary in any language. It helps us to understand even the hardest questions related to Science, Mathematics and languages. To reduce stress, we can read books. Reading also teaches us to feel what others feel through words.

Imagine, I gained self-confidence because I read about a character in a book that I could relate to and thanks to that, I was able to develop some very healthy habits.

Bill, I would advise you to make a big effort to read at least a few pages of a book every day. Reading can help you learn things and you can apply them to your life.
You can take just ten to fifteen minutes a day.
Reading is important because it opens your mind to a world of possibilities you did not even know existed. It also teaches you to put yourself in other people's shoes, because you can read a story from several people's perspectives. Also, by reading a lot, it can give you confidence.

Bill: Thanks for that advice! I will think about it.

Roxanna: Okay! I look forward to your decision.

21

Bill: It is time to go home.

23

One morning when there was no school, Bill
and his mom decided to go for a walk
in a park.

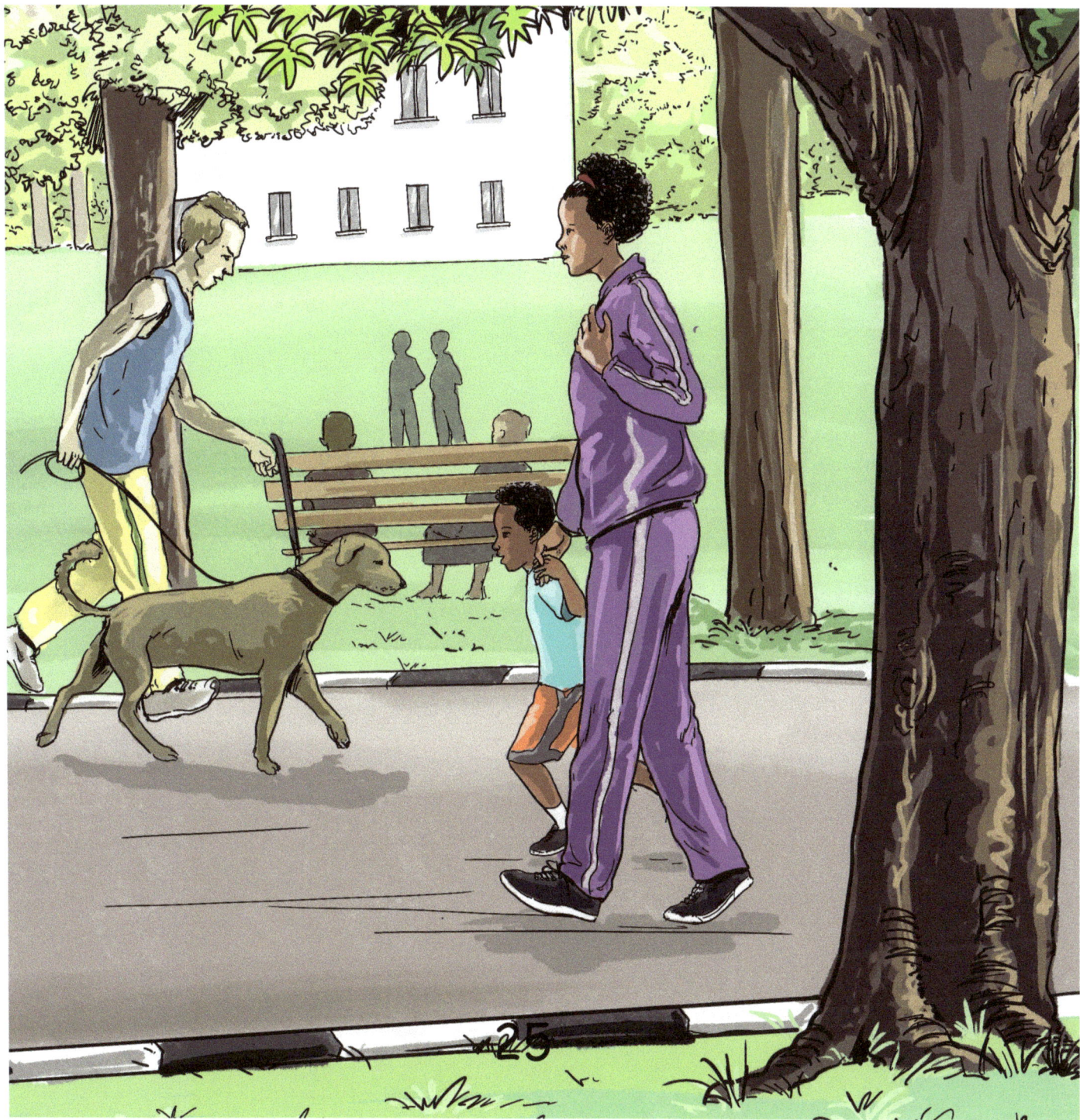

Bill: Mom, what are they doing?

27

Mom: They are reading.

Bill: Oh yes! I remember what Roxanna told me once about reading. Mom, can you also tell me why we need to read?

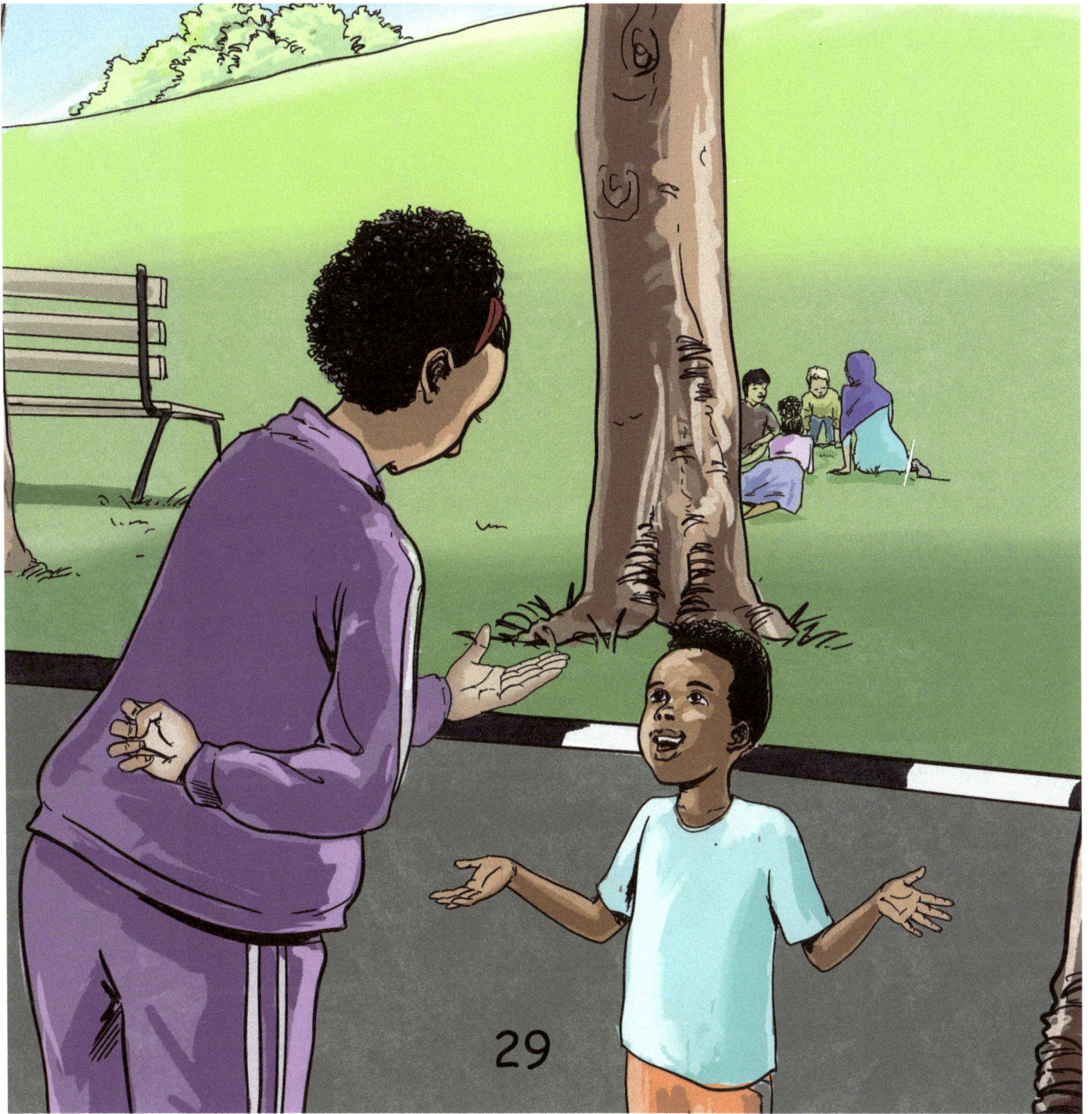

29

Mom: Bill, can you first tell me what your favourite cartoon is?

Bill: Tom the Alien!

Mom: Well! Imagine there was a book about Tom the Alien, would you read it?

Bill: I am not sure.

31

Mom: Why? When you read, you can imagine anything you want! You can also imagine that you are in the world of Tom the Alien!

Mom: Reading allows you to increase your imagination. It is much more fun than watching cartoons because with the book, you can imagine yourself in the place of Tom the Alien. Isn't that cool?

Bill: Yes, that's so much fun! What else can we do with reading, mom?

Mom: Lots of things, you can become as smart as Einstein by reading books on Science or Physics. Reading allows us to learn new words and it also allows us to go into an infinite world!

Bill: Wow, this is so cool! Mom, can we go to the public library together this afternoon to get some books?

Mom: Okay! Yes, we can go.

Bill: Thanks Mom!

PUBLIC LIBRARY

35

Mom: Be careful, we must not make any noise inside, or the librarian might get angry. We have to be quiet.

Bill: Okay, Mom!

Once inside the library, a librarian comes in.

Librarian: Hi, I am Ms. Poppy. How can I help you?

Mom: My son is looking for books.

Ms. Poppy: Ah, let me show you around. We can take a tour together.

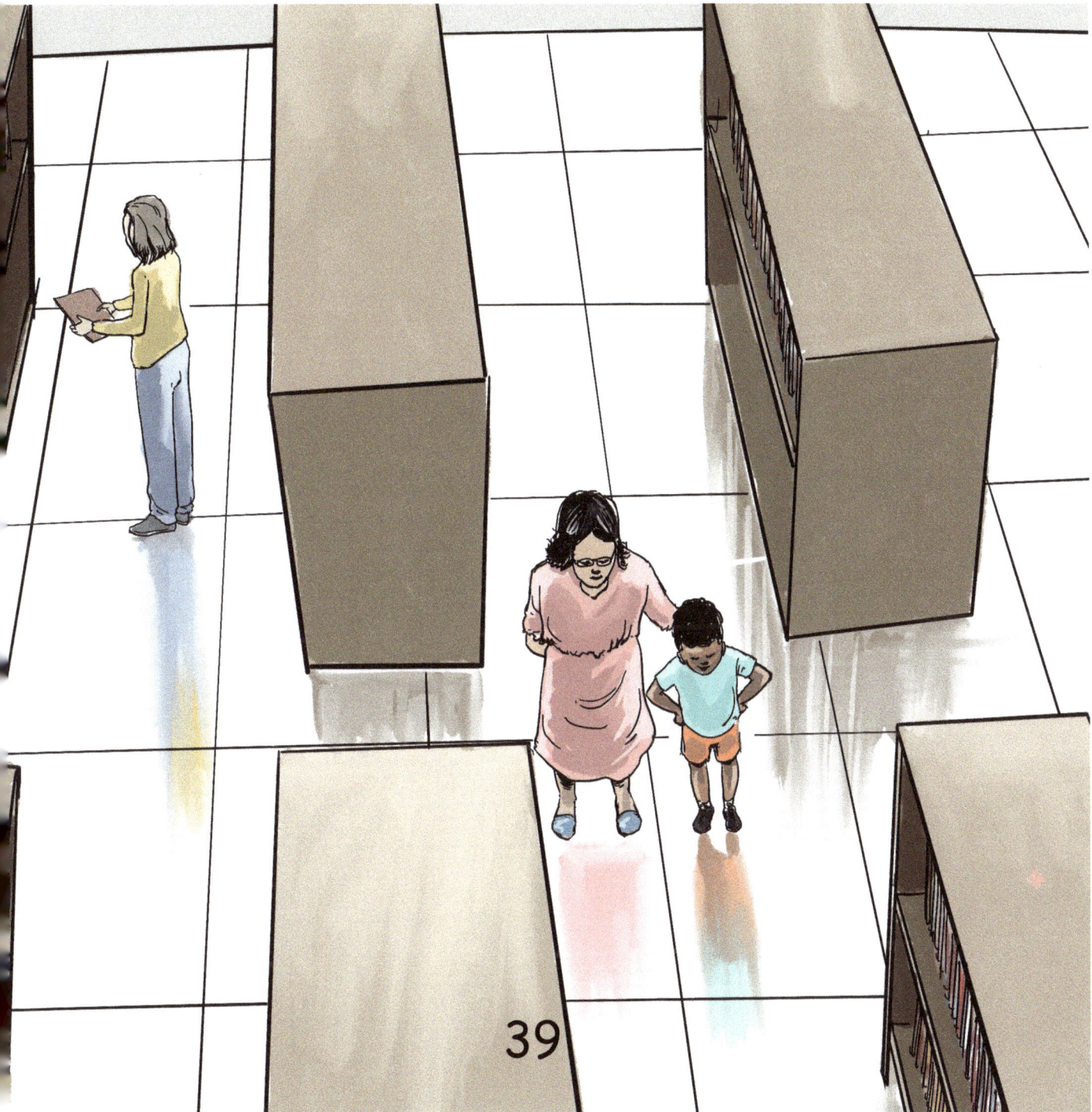

Bill: Mom, this is really big, there are a lot of books!

Ms. Poppy: Bill, what do you want to read? As you can see, there are books of all genres: science fiction, fantasy, comics, and so much more! We have different kinds of books written by different authors.

Bill: That's great! Ms. Poppy, do you have any books about aliens?

Ms. Poppy: Yes, of course! I will help you find them.

43

Bill chooses three books about aliens.

Ms. Poppy: I will put the three books into the library system. Bill, you have one week to return these books to the library. Is that okay?

Bill: Yes, it's okay!

Ms. Poppy: If you come back, you can choose other books.

Bill: Thank you, Ms. Poppy!

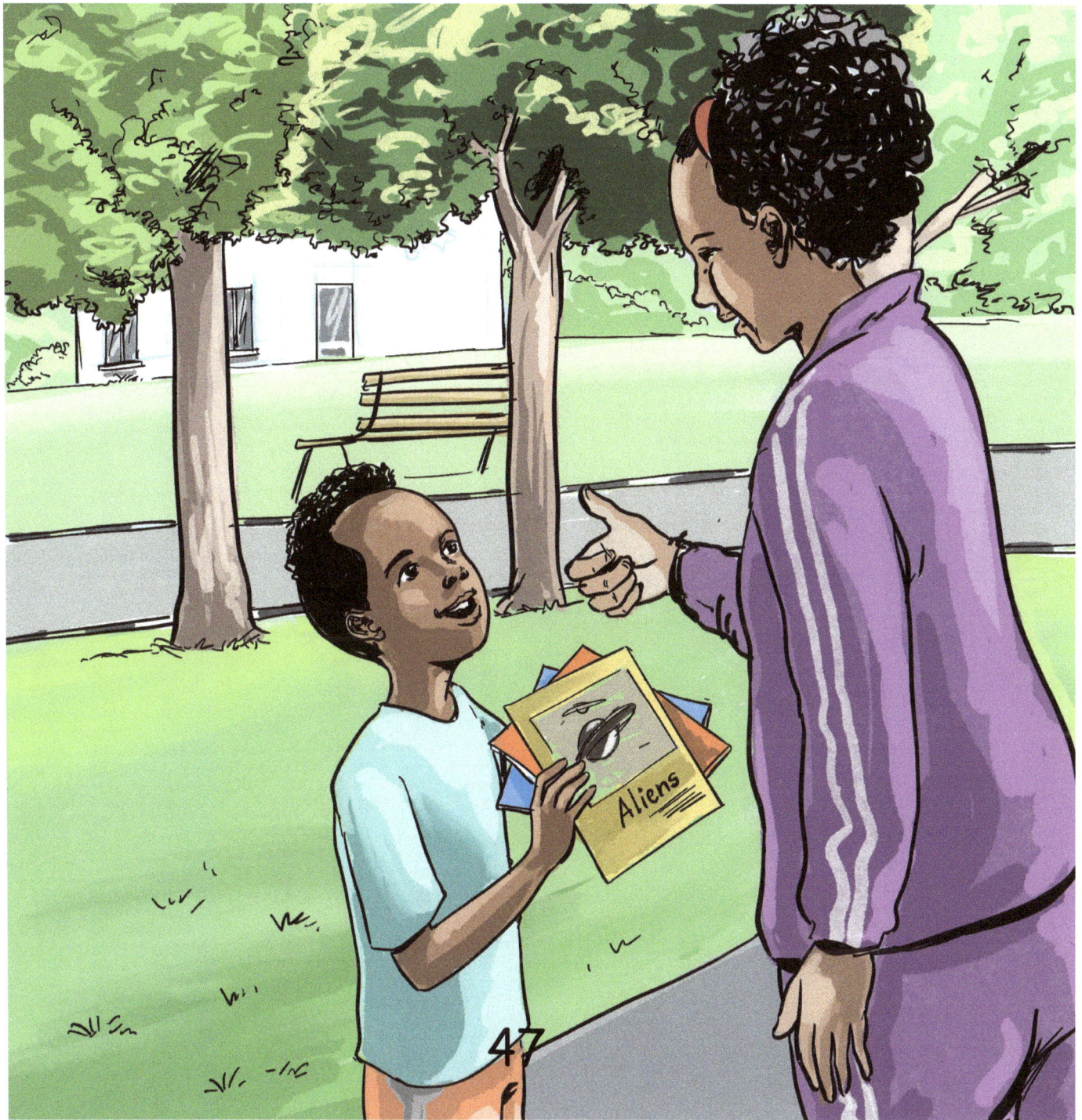

47

Mom: Well done Bill! In a few days, I am sure you will become a better reader and you will learn a lot of very interesting things. In reading, there is an incredible wealth!

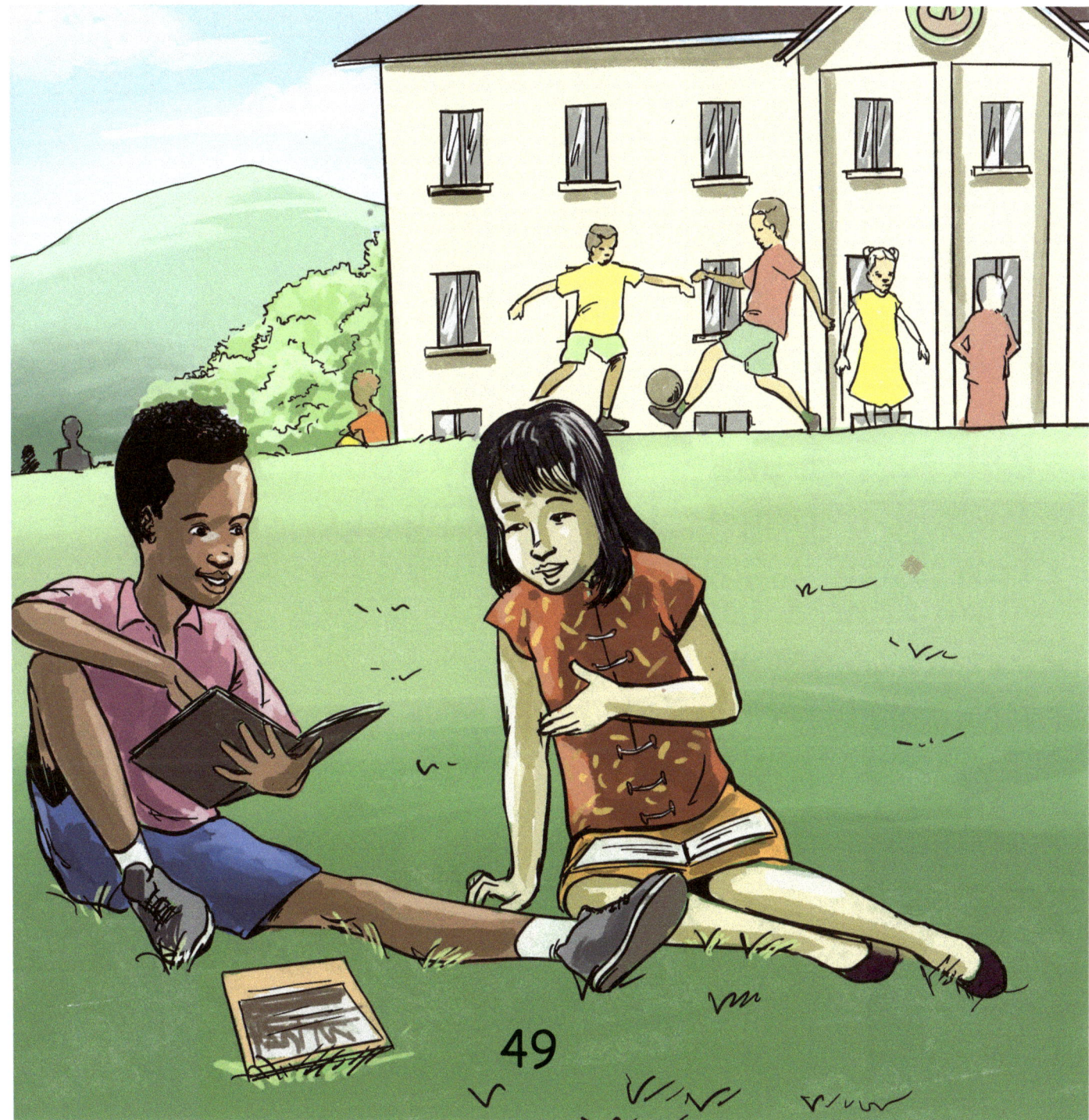

49

After a week, Bill and Roxanna meet at school.

Bill: Now I understand why you like to read. I am starting to like reading too. In the last few days, I got to read three books about aliens and I liked them.

Roxanna: I am glad that you now know the importance and wealth that comes from reading.

Title: Writing: Incredible Wealth/
written by Eugenie Mujawiyera;
illustrated by Chris Rutayisire

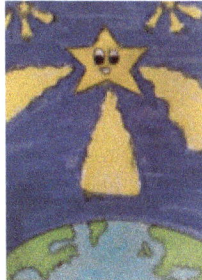

51

52

www.ingramcontent.com/pod-product-compliance
Lightning Source LLC
Chambersburg PA
CBHW040002040426
42337CB00032B/5204